The ABC's of Empowered Teams

Building Blocks for Success

By Mark Towers

SkillPath Publications
Mission, KS

Editor: Kelly Scanlon

Cover and Page Design: Sharlyn Kaye

Library of Congress Catalog Card Number: 95-71722

ISBN: 1-878-542-76-1

10 9 8   06 07 08 09

Printed in the United States of America

CONTENTS

INTRODUCTION

Walk into the business section of any bookstore today and you'll find a large number of books related to teamwork. Walk into most organizations today and you'll find slogans and pictures that emphasize the power of teams. Yes, teamwork is a hot topic these days.

Why?

Because many of the world's most effective organizations are finding out that the old concept of one boss and many workers can be replaced by the empowered team model. That's what this book is all about — reorganizing the workplace into empowered teams. Empowered teams are necessary and important in terms of organizational development. Empowered teams seem to be gaining momentum because they:

- Reduce costs.
- Improve the quality of products and services.
- Give employees more input and enhance the quality of work life.
- Increase productivity.
- Help cut absenteeism and turnover.
- Help reduce conflict.
- Enhance creativity and innovation.
- Create better adaptability and flexibility in the organization.

In 1990, Edward Lawler, director of the Center for Organizational Effectiveness at the University of Southern California, estimated that nearly 7 percent of U.S. companies were currently using some form of empowered teams. Informal estimates indicate that by the end of the decade, 50 percent of the U.S. work force may work on some kind of empowered team! Organizations that have instituted empowered teams have reported these positive examples of productivity and quality improvements:

- An insurance company reduced telephone response time from 11 minutes to 15 seconds.
- An assembly line improved its quality control by 42 percent.
- A paper mill instituted teams to achieve the most successful and profitable start-up in the history of the entire paper industry.

Yes, the fast-paced, ever-changing, quality-driven environments we work in today require more work to be done in teams. Yet, many organizations are simply giving lip service to teamwork. Many workers report that teamwork is simply a buzzword or yet another management fad. Indeed, they truthfully report that most employees are simply interested in protecting their own turf.

This struggle between team orientation and individual orientation is easily understood: America is a country of rugged individualists. In fact, 70 percent of the other cultures in the world are more team-oriented than Americans! But in spite of our cultural orientation toward individualism, global competition demands that we embrace the challenge of making today's organizations more flat and more flexible than ever before. We must rid the workplace of bureaucracies.

The organizations that survive into the twenty-first century will be characterized by a high degree of teamwork at all levels. They will have embraced the new model of participative leadership. They will exude the philosophy that participation and team empowerment is superior to hierarchy and control of the individual. Assuredly, this paradigm shift will not be an easy one; there will be some pain along the way.

The purpose of this book is to serve as your guidepost for building empowered teams. It was not designed to answer all of your questions regarding teams — that would be impossible. It was designed to stimulate your creativity so you and your organization can take action and create more teamwork around you.

> "No matter what your business, teams are the wave of the future."
> — Jerry Junkins
> CEO of Texas Instruments

A

"Restructuring should not be approached tentatively and cannot be achieved painlessly."
— Jean B. Keffeler

"A" IS FOR ALIGNMENT OF THE ORGANIZATION

Frederick Taylor, a famous American management consultant who lived from 1856 to 1915, once said, "Any change workers make to the plan is fatal to success." This kind of "us versus them" thinking, or alignment, has typified organizations for many years. Even today, many organizational charts follow an upper-level management, middle-level management, and front-line worker structure. These organizations adhere to the **POSDIC** style of management:

Plan

Organize

Staff

Direct

Inspect

Control

Management's job is to do the planning, and the employee's job is to execute the plan.

An organization characterized by empowered *teams* can change this type of alignment. What is an empowered team? An empowered team is a cohesive unit of people who enjoy the privileges of empowerment and the challenges of continuously improving the organization. Teams flatten and broaden the typical hierarchical pyramid. They help align the organization around key functions. For instance, a team can come together to discuss better ways to serve customers or to develop creative ways to save money and time. Team alignment is healthy for organizations because it gives everyone a chance to give vital input.

5

But don't be misled. Implementing empowered teams is not easy! Organizations that embrace this new style of alignment will need to change their supervision and management styles and rethink traditional bureaucratic notions of performance appraisal and reward. The old notion of POSDIC will turn to one of teaching *others* to Plan, Organize, Staff, Direct, Inspect, and Control for themselves.

This organizational realignment will be led by a committed steering team (see "S" for "Steering Team"). Several years ago, there was one supervisor for every seven employees. Currently, there is one supervisor for every 18 employees. It is estimated that by the year 2000, there will be one supervisor for every 75 employees! Taking this kind of data into account, the steering team's challenge will be to realign the organization by pushing power, knowledge, information, and rewards downward in the organization through teams.

"It is the major responsibility of management to foster the conditions that promote effective teamwork."

— *Elton Mayo*

A

"The successful organization has already moved from hierarchy and control to democracy and participation."
— *Charles Garfield*

"B" IS FOR BOUNDARIES

Athletic teams have boundaries — rules that govern the behavior of the teams. Before any athletic contest begins, the officials explain these boundaries. For instance, in a baseball game, both teams know what constitutes a foul ball and a home run. The teams must stay inside the boundaries and play by the rules in order to be successful. The same is true for empowered workplace teams.

The job of upper-level management is to clearly state the boundaries of empowered teams. All empowered teams in a team-driven work environment are governed by a steering team, which is a group of individuals who are put in place by upper-level management. The steering team's job is to remove interference for empowered work teams, support them, listen to them, and set boundaries for them. These boundaries will restrict, guide, and create a level of comfort for team members by giving them guidelines from which they must operate. (See "S" for more information on steering teams.)

Teams may be able to spend only so much money and time on a project, for example. Teams in one organization in upstate New York have a boundary of $50,000! If a decision facing the team exceeds the amount of $50,000, the team must get permission from upper-level management in order to proceed.

In turn, each empowered team needs to set its own ground rules, expectations, or boundaries. Teams often brainstorm these rules at the very beginning of the team's formation. They are written down and posted for all team members to see. These ground rules create a feeling of safety for team members so the team's work can be done.

Some examples of solid ground rules that empowered work teams use include:

1. Listen constructively. Only one person can talk at a time.
2. Be on time.
3. If in doubt, check it out. Don't make negative assumptions about one another.
4. Don't hoard information — share it.
5. Don't lose faith in one another.
6. Insist on consensus.
7. Have fun.

"Communication
is about power
and power is about
boundaries."
— *Anonymous*

"Creative minds always

have been known to

survive any kind of

bad training."

— Anna Freud

"C" IS FOR CREATIVITY

The challenge for today's businesses is to keep costs down, maximize human potential, and show profitability and viability in both the profit and not-for-profit sectors. This can only be accomplished through creativity. Teams lend themselves to the creative endeavor.

Dr. Harold Stevenson at the University of Michigan has been comparing elementary and secondary schools in the United States and other cultures for more than a decade. In his research, Stevenson has found that students in some nations are more advanced than those in the United States. Furthermore, he has found that their curriculum is not characterized by rote memorization. Surprisingly, he has found that these students enjoy more recess periods and more time to play at school. Overall, Dr. Stevenson found that they enjoy school more and are less stressed by school than American children.

Although there are several factors that account for the superior performance of these students, Stevenson and his colleagues were most amazed by the differences in teaching styles. Some of the teachers in these countries spend as little as three hours a day in a classroom, spending the rest of the day preparing lessons, discussing educational strategies with their fellow educators, and working with small groups of students who need tutoring.

Note the emphasis on teamwork! It is a predominant part of the culture of these schools, and it's producing superior results. Dialogue is the key. The teachers are dialoguing with one another and then dialoguing even more with small teams of students. Stevenson says these teachers regard their students as active participants in the learning process. They play an important role in producing, explaining, and evaluating solutions to problems.

Conversely, many American teachers are "Lone Ranger" types. They prepare their lessons individually, and most want control over their classrooms.

It doesn't take a rocket scientist to figure out that teams enhance creativity in school as well as in the workplace. Jack Welch, the tremendously charismatic CEO of General Electric, has said, "We tear all the walls down and put teams from all functions in one room to bring new products to life. One room, one coffeepot, one team, one shared mission. That's how GE developed advanced ultrasound products and its GE90 jet engine. Before long, it will be the way GE develops everything."

"You must have chaos within
you to give birth to a
rising star."
— *Nietzche*

"We need to find ways to capture the creative and innovative spirit of the American worker. That's the real organizational challenge."

— *Paul Allaire*

"D" IS FOR DESIRED SIZE

The size of teams will vary from organization to organization — and even within organizations. Every organization is unique. What works at Disney probably won't work at Xerox. What works in Anniston, Alabama, may not work in Anchorage, Alaska.

But if you want a bite-sized rule of thumb to follow, here it is: The best size for a team is **7**, plus or minus **2** people, but never more than **12**. This guideline for team size comes from insightful research done at Ohio State University in the mid-1980s.

Remember, this is a rule of thumb. Some teams function quite nicely with more members, others with fewer. So don't live and die by this rule. Just use it as a guideline.

"None of us is as smart as all of us."
                                    — Ray Kroc

"E" IS FOR EMPOWERMENT

In some organizations, *empowerment* is nothing more than a buzzword. People may espouse its principles but never put them into practice. In these organizations, the concept has no significance or value. But consider what can be accomplished in an organization that truly empowers its employees.

There was a severe winter storm in the western part of America. Phone service was interrupted. At Federal Express, no deliveries could be made. But, of course, Federal Express has a commitment to overnight delivery.

A nonmanagement employee drove to the phone company to find out what he could do about the phone lines being down. The phone company explained that it would take at least three days to reattach the downed lines to the transformer, which was on top of a mountain outside of town.

Not to be deterred, the employee drove to the top of the mountain to see whether he could fix the problem. The snow was too deep and he was unable to reach the top of the mountain, so he returned to town and rented a helicopter to fly him to the top! The pilot could not find a place to land, so the employee jumped out of the helicopter into a snowdrift. He then proceeded to hook up the phone lines. Now that's an empowered employee!

Let's examine this employee's decision with regard to three key questions relating to empowerment.

QUESTION #1:   For the sake of myself and the team, is this decision safe?

19

In this dramatic example, the Federal Express employee did take some risks. Obviously, he had some working knowledge about phone lines and electricity in order to undertake this challenge. But he must have felt he was not endangering his life or anyone else's as he proceeded to hook up the phone lines. On a daily basis, most decisions will obviously not involve nearly as much energy or daring.

QUESTION #2: Is this good for my team or organization in the long run (not necessarily the short run)?

The Federal Express employee felt responsible for Federal Express and its reputation. His long-term loyalty to team is what makes this story so strong. He sacrificed time, energy, and money in the short run to perpetuate Federal Express and its long-term commitment to customers.

QUESTION #3: Does the action I'm about to take project a sense of caring to our customer(s)?

The Federal Express employee aimed to delight his customer. He not only wanted the external customer to be happy, he also had to feel a sense of loyalty to his internal customer — his fellow team members at Federal Express.

There you have it. Three key questions that define the boundaries of empowerment. Yes, sometimes empowered employees will push those boundaries. But pushing boundaries is what turns mediocre organizations into great organizations.

"What we have to do now is figure out a way to get people to make broad contributions to their companies."

— Nancy Austin

"F" IS FOR
FOOD AND FUN

Food is a symbol of acceptance. Traditionally, people are offered food and drink when they enter someone's home. This offering helps breaks down barriers that have been put up to "wall people off" from one another.

Teams do need to eat together — at least periodically. The bonding that occurs through conversation and laughter while people eat together is definitely worth the investment.

Most assuredly, teams need to be task-oriented. They must get work done; they must be seen as productive.

But just as important, team members need to eat, laugh, and celebrate with one another. When the social orientation of teams dies, the task orientation dies soon after.

> "No man is a failure who is enjoying life."
> — William Feather

"To travel hopefully is

better than

to arrive."

— *Sir James Jeans*

"G" IS FOR GEESE

Geese are interesting creatures. They truly know how to create an effective and efficient empowered team. Their natural ability to model "shared leadership" within a team is a phenomenon that deserves further scrutiny by human beings.

Let's consider these observations that wildlife experts have made about geese. Notice how the actions of the geese in flight provide a positive model for empowered teams.

EXAMPLE #1: Geese fly in a "V" formation. Flying in this pattern enables them to migrate 60 to 70 percent farther than if each bird flew unaccompanied. As each goose flaps its wings, it creates less wind resistance for the bird following it in the V formation.

INSIGHT #1: Team is an acronym for Together Everyone Achieves More. Like the geese, people can truly live this philosophy too. Indeed, sharing a common vision, sharing a common direction, and supporting one another can enable the team to achieve great things.

EXAMPLE #2: Obviously, a V-shaped formation requires that there be a lead goose where the two lines of geese come together. The lead goose is not always the same bird. Most of the geese take a turn on the point or lead position. When the lead goose begins to tire, it moves back to a regular support position along one of the lines of the V. Another goose then rotates into the point position and takes its turn fighting into the wind and leading the flock from the point position.

INSIGHT #2: It pays to rotate leadership. By rotating leadership, more than one individual on the team gets a chance to grow and expand his or her skill base. Furthermore, team members don't have to depend on one person always being the leader.

EXAMPLE #3: Some geese stay inside the V structure. These geese are too old or too weak to take their turn at the front of the V formation or in a support position along either line of the V formation.

INSIGHT #3: We have to understand people's strengths and weaknesses within a team framework. We must look for each person to contribute to the best of his or her ability.

EXAMPLE #4: Geese honk as they fly. However, observers of geese tell us that the lead goose (the one on the point) never honks. Wildlife observers theorize that the geese behind the leader honk praise, encouragement, and support to the lead goose.

INSIGHT #4: Recognition, praise, and encouragement are the glue that holds and bonds teams together.

EXAMPLE #5: Invariably, a goose may feel a need to leave the formation and go down to the ground. Perhaps the goose feels ill, has been wounded, or needs a drink of water. When this happens, two other geese leave the formation and escort this goose to the ground. They go with this bird in order to protect and support it. These escort geese will stay with the goose until it dies. If it does not die, the escort geese help the goose return to the formation or they find another formation of geese to join.

INSIGHT #5: When times are tough, team members need to support one another. Teamwork requires commitment through the "rough patches" as well as the good times.

EXAMPLE #6:	There are always a few geese (or perhaps one goose) that are flying by themselves a few yards away from the V formation. Experts believe that these geese are scouting for a better wind current or a more productive way for the flock to travel.
INSIGHT #6:	Teams must adhere to the notion that there is always a way to work smarter rather than work harder. The notion of constant improvement through teamwork is the essence of creating a quality organization.

It is truly remarkable that these wild animals have been genetically programmed to work so well together as a team. As we create empowered teams within the workplace, the geese continue to serve as terrific role models for success.

"Our duty is to not see through one another, but to see one another through."
— Anonymous

"One should
sympathize with the
joy, the beauty, the
color of life — the
less said about life's
sores the better."
— Oscar Wilde

"H" IS FOR HUMOR

It's no secret that all work and no play makes employees unhappy and unproductive. In fact, Dr. William Frey, a prominent researcher and professor at Stanford University, has studied laughter and its effect on human health for several years. He and others in the medical field have called laughter "internal jogging." Laughter is good for the heart muscles and diaphragm and massages many internal organs. Dr. Frey recommends that we laugh at least fifteen times a day.

Obviously, none of us can afford to turn into total clowns at work. There must always be balance. But we can make work a more enjoyable place to be. Humor and fun in the workplace can help increase productivity, enhance loyalty to the organization, fend off stress, stimulate creativity, and promote enthusiasm.

Indeed, teamwork and humor go hand in hand. The camaraderie that is so essential to teamwork is created most quickly when people laugh and play together.

Here are some ways to bring laughter, play, and humor into your work teams:

- **Keep a camera in your desk.** Take an occasional picture of a silly mistake someone makes or an impromptu celebration.

- **Create a contest.** Start a weight-loss contest, a quickest-to-answer-the-phone contest, a guess-the-baby-picture contest, or a great-idea-of-the-week contest. The possibilities are endless. Think about what you do during team meetings. Find a way to turn some routine part of your meeting into a contest. Give creative and inexpensive prizes to the winner(s). Also give fun prizes to those who do not win.

- **Have a raffle.** Ask a nearby restaurant manager to donate a free meal or dessert to your work team(s). Have a drawing and give it away at the end of an appropriate meeting.
- **Buy some crazy props at a toy store or novelty shop.** Keep them in your desk. When the timing is appropriate, pull one out. Some suggestions: a bottle of bubbles, a water pistol, or a mask.
- **Buy a humorous audiocassette tape.** Circulate it among team members.
- **Take a humor break during team meetings.** At each meeting, have one person relate a humorous or embarrassing moment from their past.

In terms of its ability to build team cohesiveness, humor is much like food. Both satisfy the social orientation of teams. Most assuredly, teams must strike a balance between their task (goal and achievement) orientation as well as their social (nourishing and caring) orientation.

The human being is the only animal that laughs. Our job is not to figure out why that is so. Our job is to consciously encourage laughter, play, and humor. But more important, our job is to lead by example and to get our quota of fifteen laughs each day. Enjoy!

"We don't laugh because

we're happy. We're happy

because we laugh."

— *William James*

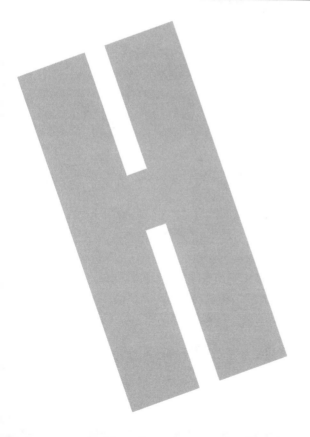

"I" IS FOR IMPASSE

Teams often struggle as they strive to reach consensus on critical issues. Teams that can't reach a consensus are said to have reached an *impasse* — a predicament from which there is no obvious escape.

When teams reach an impasse, leadership must prevail. Lee Iacocca is one leader who seems to be extremely skilled at getting teams beyond impasse. In his biography, he shares his formula for dealing with teams that stall on an issue. As the team leader, he says he would look at his team members and ask three questions:

1. Does everyone understand the big picture?
2. Do you understand your specific role in the big picture?
3. What can I personally do to help you achieve your role within this big picture?

This simplistic and service-oriented leadership style is exactly what is needed to get teams moving when they are struggling. Often, as leaders, we must back up and reassess the mission, focus, and goal of the team.

This reassessment or "time out" allows people to address and clarify the three critical notions that face any team during impasse:

1. What is our purpose?
2. What do you expect from the team leader(s)?
3. What do you expect from the team member(s)?

If a team cannot resolve these issues, then forming a new team may become the only viable option. Someone once said, "Either live with it, lobby, or leave." If the team cannot come to consensus regarding critical issues, then it may be time to start over.

"There are two ways
of spreading light: to
be the candle or the
mirror that
reflects it."
— *Edith Wharton*

"My interest is in the future because I'm going to spend the rest of my life there."
— *Charles F. Kettering*

"Life is like playing a violin in public and learning the instrument as one goes on."
— Samuel Butler

"J" IS FOR JOURNEY

When teams are formed, they come together as one to embark on a complex journey. Although social scientists cannot prescribe an *exact* model of a team's journey, most theorists of team development adhere to the simple, hands-on model of team development (a team's journey, if you will) called forming, storming, norming, and performing. There is one final stage of team development that is seldom addressed. It is referred to as disbanding.

Let's take a graphic view of a team's journey before describing each stage of development:

During **Stage One,** or the forming stage, team participants are excited. They like the idea of being on a team. They look forward to team meetings. The uncertainty of what lies before them sparks their curiosity.

During **Stage Two,** or the storming stage, team participants may confront one another. They may argue with one another or challenge the team's goals. This storming stage is sometimes described as painful.

Recently, someone expressed concern about her team by saying, "Things were progressing beautifully and then we slipped back to the storming stage again." But civilized disagreement is simply part of a team's development. It is worth remembering this concept in order to effectively deal with storming: "If we both agree, then one of us isn't necessary."

During **Stage Three,** or the norming stage, team participants begin to jell as a functioning unit. They begin to feel comfortable with one another and to accept one another. Team loyalty is enhanced and accented during this stage. Team participants are able to air common concerns and share their feelings with one another.

Team members begin to have more fun together, may get together outside of team meetings, and begin showing solidarity in other ways, such as wearing team T-shirts. During this stage, the time, money, and energy invested in teams finally begins to pay dividends.

During **Stage Four,** or the performing stage, team participants are "hitting on all cylinders" as a unit. They begin functioning like a flock of geese (see "G" for "Geese"). They are able to share leadership with one another and delegate assignments. They truly come together as a team.

Eventually, fully-functioning teams must disband. This **fifth and final stage** may be painful for many team members. As successful teams disband, some teams throw parties. Others have luncheons. Some give awards.

But the team members have been transformed forever. They carry with them a new set of experiences and a new set of skills into other arenas. They look for and find new opportunities for team development. New journeys await them and the process of forming, storming, norming, performing, and disbanding continues.

A team's journey could aptly be described as a drama or perhaps as a dance. Teams do definitely "dance" among these various stages of development — depending on the issue at hand, the mood of the key players, small victories and setbacks, and so forth.

Let's remember that from this dance comes the strength, hope, and vision for dealing with the challenges we all face. As workplace issues and life in general become increasingly more complex, the next generation will require an even greater investment in teamwork. It is our job to leave them a legacy. We must show them how to come together as teams and to truly succeed as members of a team — not simply as individuals.

"Although there is clearly no path for establishing a high performance, high commitment work team system, the conception, design implementation, and day-to-day management of this kind of work system requires consistent and continuous attention."
— Robert Sherwood

"Life means to have
something definite to
do — a mission to fulfill —
and in the measure in
which we avoid setting our
life to something, we make
it empty. Human life, by its
very nature, has to be
dedicated to something."
— *Jose Ortega Y Gasset*

"K" IS FOR KEEP THE FOCUS ON RESULTS

In 1988, a large American financial institution launched a "total quality" program to improve itself and win more customers. The company trainers trained hundreds of people and predicted the program's eventual success. Two years later, in 1990, the program's consultants summarized the progress of the company.

They wrote: "We have forty-eight teams up and running. The morale of the employees regarding the TQM program is very positive. However, we do not have any bottom-line performance improvements to report."

This is disheartening. People do get excited about change, but they don't get *committed* to a program unless it achieves bottom-line results. Therefore, every team needs to commission itself with at least one RM-SMART goal.

The **SMART** portion of the **RM-SMART** formula stands for these goal characteristics:

- **Specific**
- **Measurable**
- **Attainable**
- **Realistic**
- **Time-framed**

The **RM** portion of the formula is short for Road Map. A team can stay even more focused by breaking down its SMART goal(s) into smaller chunks, or a written road map, during the forming stage of team development (see "J" for "Journey"). By following this Road Map, the team will be able to stay on target, execute effectively, and hopefully produce the desired results.

Let's examine how the process of setting a SMART goal actually works. First, an empowered team agrees to set this SMART goal: We will reduce customer complaints by 60 percent by the end of this calendar year. Indeed, this goal meets all of the criteria for setting a **SMART** goal. It is:

- **S**pecific.
- **M**easurable.
- **A**ttainable (collectively, they feel it is).
- **R**ealistic (collectively, they feel it is).
- **T**ime-framed.

Next, "the rubber meets the road" when the team creates its road map. Indeed, a road map is a detailed plan of action that gives the team direction. It involves breaking the SMART goal into smaller, doable tasks that enable the team to drive toward its goal of reducing customer complaints.

In this case, the team might create a written plan similar to the one in the following example.

THE ROAD MAP

Task 1: Jerry and Donna will examine all customer complaint sheets and analyze them regarding the most common patterns. They will report back to the team by April 3.

Task 2: Bill and Linda will conduct a focus group that consists of our key customers (our larger accounts). They will invite them to the office and ask them to share their complaints and their suggestions regarding how we can provide better service.

Task 3: After gathering this information, we will get consensus regarding our plan of action. We will then approach upper-level management with our suggestions. We will emphasize facts, figures, and the actions that must be taken in order to reach our SMART goal. We will approach them with a written plan by July 12.

Task 4: We will kick off and implement our new plan on August 4.

Task 5: Sue and Lyle will be in charge of monitoring our new systems. They will collect data and give us a report by September 21.

Task 6: The entire team will meet every two weeks to discuss and monitor our efforts. Sue and Lyle will be in charge of constantly improving our customer service and reducing complaints.

Task 7: The team will issue a formal report to upper-level management on December 22. Donna and Bill will write the final report.

Task 8: We will have a meeting with upper-level management on December 28 regarding our efforts.

> **"Who begins too much accomplishes little."**
>
> **— German proverb**

"Good communication
is as stimulating as
black coffee, and
just as hard to
sleep after."
— *Anne Morrow*
Lindbergh

"L" IS FOR LEVELS
OF COMMUNICATION

Think about a recent conversation you had with another person that lasted for at least five minutes. Now, analyze it by answering these four questions about the conversation:

1. For what portion of the conversation did I simply tell the other person what he or she wanted to hear?

    Rate yourself from 0-100% _____%

2. For what portion of the conversation did I tell the other person what I thought?

    Rate yourself from 0-100% _____%

3. For what portion of the conversation did I tell the other person what I felt?

    Rate yourself from 0-100% _____%

4. For what portion of the conversation did I tell the other person what was in my "gut"?

    Rate yourself from 0-100% _____%

These four questions represent the four levels of communication. Each level is explained in detail below.

Level 1:   *Telling the other person what he or she simply wants to hear.* "Jeremy, of course I think that new approach will work." (You may have doubts that it will work, but you don't take the time to share them with Jeremy.)

Level 2:   *Telling the other person what you think.* "Jeremy, I think you may want to examine the planning behind that new approach; it may need some more detail." (Here, you take the time to express a thought and to "shoot straight" with Jeremy.)

Level 3:	Telling the other person how you feel. "Jeremy, I feel that this new approach will create too much chaos and resentment for me as well as for other people in this department." (Here, you take the time to express yourself from a deeper, more intuitive level. You send Jeremy a message that includes thoughts as well as feelings.)
Level 4:	Telling the other person what is in your gut. "Jeremy, I've spent the last nine years of my life working in this department. I have some very strong feelings about this new approach, and I want you to hear me out on these concerns." (Here, you let Jeremy know that you have a strong and vested emotional interest in the situation.)

Fully-functioning teams encourage and support deeper levels of communication. They encourage team members to go beyond Stage One, or simply telling people what they want to hear in order to appease them.

Effective team leaders demonstrate leadership by establishing a "safe" place in which all team members can communicate at any of these four levels (see "B" for "Boundaries"). Yes, it's okay for people to speak their minds. Encourage it!

By doing so, your team will come up with fuller and richer ideas. These ideas will transform the organization. As the organization transforms itself, teams become more imbedded and ingrained within the culture of the organization. The cycle of teams repeats itself, the organization effectively deals with change, and your organization becomes an exciting, fun, and educational place in which to work.

"Silence gives consent,
or a horrible feeling
that nobody's
listening."

— *Franklin P. Jones*

"An individual without information cannot
take responsibility; an individual who is
given information cannot help but
take responsibility."

— Jan Carlson
CEO, Scandinavian Airlines

"M" IS FOR MEETINGS

Just a few short years ago it was popular for some business consultants to say, "The best size for a committee to be is one." This statement summed up the feelings of many people who were tired of spending time in unproductive team meetings.

On the other hand, there is nothing more exciting and more pertinent than a well-run, *productive* team meeting. In fact, as more and more organizations embrace the team concept, there will be *more* meetings. It's an unavoidable part of the process. The key is to ensure that the meetings are productive. The elements of an effective team meeting are represented in the acronym **"SLAP."**

"S" is a reminder to *start on time* — no matter what! Don't wait on anybody — not even the boss. Promptness is a virtue. Notre Dame's Lou Holtz says: "I normally will walk into a meeting at precisely the proper time. The first thing we do on a continuous basis is set our watches. We go by LLH time. This stands for 'Louis Leo Holtz' time."

"L" is a reminder to *limit* the amount of time you spend in any team meeting to ninety minutes or less. After ninety minutes, the law of diminishing returns assumes control; people have other things on their minds — their own paperwork, phone calls they need to return, deadlines, and so forth.

Furthermore, push to end meetings just a bit early. Everyone likes effectiveness and efficiency. Ending early gives team participants a "cushion" of time. They get a chance to breathe before switching gears into the next item on their "To Do" list.

"A" is a reminder to follow a carefully planned *agenda*.

Remember to put the toughest item first. An old saying is applicable here: "If you've got a lot of frogs to eat, eat the biggest one first."

"P" is a reminder to have a *purpose*. Make certain that the meeting has an overall theme. Meeting for the sake of meeting can drive folks crazy. It is estimated that 40 percent of meetings in corporate America are absolute wastes of time. Indeed, good planning on the front end of the meeting can help the team focus.

Live by the **"SLAP"** principles. Make sure everyone else on your team knows them too.

Start on time!

Limit the meeting time.

Agenda that is carefully planned

Purpose

"In a staff meeting, the supervisor is a leader, observer, expediter, questioner, and decision-maker. Please note that the role of lecturer is not listed. A supervisor should never use staff meetings to pontificate."

— *Andrew S. Grove*

"By perseverance
the snail reached
the ark."
— *Charles Haddon
Spurgeon*

"N" IS FOR NEVER BACKING UP

When upper-level management decides to institute empowered work teams, they send a powerful message to the employees within the organization. The message is clear: We are going to entrust and empower you to work in an exciting new way.

Teams are going to hit some rough patches (see "J" for Journey). When they do, don't bail out. Don't scrap the team movement. Don't throw your hands up in the air and shout: "This team stuff doesn't work! We're going back to the old way of doing things around here!"

When upper-level management decides to scrap an employee empowerment movement, it sends a dreadful message to all employees: "We don't think you have the brains to handle the decisions we are asking you to make. Furthermore, we can't trust you with increased levels of involvement and power."

Studies show that many organizations scrap a team empowerment program before eighteen months have elapsed. This is unfortunate because it takes two-and-a-half to three years for employees to become comfortable with the new approach. Like any project worth undertaking, implementing empowered teams takes time. The trick is to evolve the teams. Start slowly with one or two pilot teams and avoid excessive activity. Nurse the teams along. Make sure people get the proper training. More important, make sure people tackle meaningful and visible issues.

Support, coach, mentor, facilitate, and teach — but don't push the panic button! Remain optimistic during the tough times as your organization makes the transition to empowered teams. Perseverance is truly the key here.

"The truth is more

important than

the facts."

— *Frank Lloyd Wright*

"O" IS FOR OUTSIDE OBSERVERS

Recently, the CEO of a very successful company said: "Our organization is naked. Everything can be inspected. We don't want there to be any secrets around here." He fervently believes in letting his managers invite consultants, competitors, and various outside observers into his company to watch the organization's teams at work.

He invites the oral and written feedback of these outside observers, and he wants all his employees to get used to being role models for others. When asked whether he might be giving away his competitive advantage in the marketplace, he replied: "Walt Disney never worried about people stealing his ideas. He always felt ideas were limitless. He felt he could always find more ideas, and I feel the same way."

This kind of corporate openness is both rare and refreshing. It openly invites and stimulates creativity and growth. The point here is a simple one: Teams do not often have insight into their own behavior. They may interact and make decisions as a matter of habit. When teams are stagnant or could simply use a boost, invite "fresh and educated eyeballs" in to watch the process. These can be fellow managers and employees or Ph.D.s from a nearby university.

Have them study the team's processes and interactions. Consider the data they give you. Share it with all the team members. These types of "tweaks and nudges" from outside observers can often prod teams to produce at the next highest level.

"Excellent firms don't
believe in excellence —
only in constant
improvement and
constant change."

— *Tom Peters*

"P" IS FOR PERFORMANCE APPRAISAL

The late Dr. W. Edwards Deming, the guru of the Total Quality Management movement, asserted that the typical management appraisal of an individual employee is a short-term, initiative-killing exercise that poisons the workplace. Many others agree with him. The challenge is a clear one: In order to produce more teamwork within organizations, we must effectively and simultaneously appraise individual achievement as well as contribution to the team.

How can that be accomplished? What vehicle can replace the standard manager-subordinate appraisal system? The answer is not easy. It can come only from an empowered group of employees representing a diagonal slice of the organization. A team composed of a diagonal slice of the organization would consist of employees with various rank, degrees of power, and influence. A concerted effort would be made to make such a team representative of employees throughout the organization. For instance, an empowered team could consist of two upper-level managers, two middle managers, and two front-line workers.

These employees must convene and set a SMART goal (see "K" for "Keep the Focus on Results") of reforming the appraisal system.

Here are some ideas that will provide some guidance for a team that is struggling to revise its organization's performance appraisals:

First, always remember to retain a balance between individual achievement and team achievement.

Second, bear in mind that there are only four ways in which any employee can be appraised:

1. By his or her manager
2. By co-workers
3. By customers
4. Through self-evaluation

The team must get input from many angles regarding these issues, take good notes, realize there won't be a perfect way of doing it, and recommend something they feel upper-level management will accept. Like any other program, the original concept will be adjusted to fit the needs of the organization.

Third, many organizations (particularly in the manufacturing arena) have gone to an "if you learn more, you earn more" concept. In other words, they base appraisal and bonuses (see "R" for "Rewards") on how many different functions or jobs an employee can perform.

For instance, a General Electric plant in Bayamon, Puerto Rico, recently instituted a "Pay for Knowledge, Pay for Skills" approach. Every six months, employees rotate to different job tasks. Furthermore, employees are required to enroll in and successfully complete specifically designed vocational courses related to their jobs. As the employees gain proficiency and knowledge, they are paid more. With these types of systems in place, the work force becomes a large knowledge-based team capable of performing all tasks throughout the business.

Obviously, a great deal of work must go into the design of these systems, and even more energy is required to keep them running smoothly. But the payoffs are clear:

1. A flatter and more flexible organization
2. A work force that is not stagnant but ever-growing and ever-changing to meet the changing demands of the marketplace
3. Empowered employees who feel a greater degree of ownership

"Life teaches us to be less harsh with ourselves and with others."

— *Goethe*

"Total Quality Management is not the management of quality. It is the quality of management."
— Dr. David Garvin

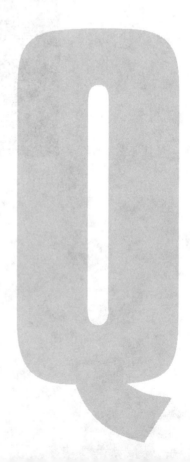

"Q" IS FOR THE QUALITY MOVEMENT

The Quality Movement in America has spurred organizations to reexamine how they operate. Visionary managers have used the TQM initiative to help people push power, knowledge, information, and rewards downward in the system through teamwork.

In keeping with the Quality Movement, teams should be primarily concerned with these four issues:

1. Better ways to delight or dazzle internal and external customers
2. Better ways to simplify and improve work processes
3. Better ways to empower all employees
4. Better ways to share critical information with employees so they can feel a greater sense of organizational ownership

Some people feel that TQM is nothing more than a panacea. (One cynic stated that TQM means "Time to Quit and Move On.") But it is not a panacea. TQM is simply a catalyst for change. It initiated the quality movement, and that movement will continue to evolve. Empowered teams will continue to be the vehicle for change as organizations move into the twenty-first century.

"Never tell people
how to do things. Tell
them what to do and
they will surprise you
with their ingenuity."

— *George S. Patton*

"R" IS FOR REWARDS

Stories about executive pay consistently make headlines in the United States. Multimillionaires often remain in control as their companies lose market share and lay off employees. Visionary managers believe that sharing some of the wealth with employees across the board creates greater employee involvement, pride, and ownership.

Consider the concept of gain sharing and the Dallas Cowboys. After winning the Super Bowl in 1993, each player was awarded $50,000. This included first-, second-, and third-team players. The chaplain also received the same amount of money.

Pushing power, knowledge, information, and rewards downward within the organization helps put an organization on the "cutting edge" in terms of organizational structure and development. Of these four variables, the sharing of rewards is most often referred to as one of the toughest challenges for a cross-functional work team to tackle. Yes, people can get touchy about their paychecks.

In order for a team to address the issues of performance appraisals (see "P" for "Performance Appraisals") and rewards, teams need to have addressed and had success with less challenging issues first (see "Y" for "Yes Within 90 Days").

There is no cookbook formula for how people should be recognized and rewarded, but again, the answer needs to come from a work team that represents a diagonal slice of the organization. Here are some ideas that an empowered work team can use as a springboard for dynamic and exciting discussion about recognition and rewards:

1. Set an employee's base salary at "X" amount (based upon a person's education level, background, etc.) Tie the rest of the person's salary (a smaller amount) to the organization's overall profits, customer satisfaction, or the employee's educational attainment (see "P" for "Performance Appraisals" and the reference to General Electric).

2. Accept the fact that front-line people can potentially make as much money as managers.

3. Upper-level management may not be ready to let a team address the issue of pay. However, there are other positive rewards besides money. In terms of looking at a generic list of motivators that could be considered a carrot (not a stick) and openly discussed, examine this list of positive strokes:
   - Recognition (trophies, T-shirts, etc.)
   - Time off (flex time, etc.)
   - Food
   - Autonomy (advancement)
   - Personal growth experience
   - Prizes (raffles, etc.)
   - Fun (parties, etc.)
   - Helping others (doing volunteer work, etc.)

Add to this list based upon your past experiences and your team discussions.

The intent of discussing rewards is not to castigate management. It is not to create a socialistic and "everybody is equal around here" type of work environment. The purpose of discussing rewards is to stretch and grow the organization and the people in it by distributing realistic rewards within the existing workplace.

"After you've done a thing the same way for two years, look it over carefully. After five years, look at it with suspicion. After ten years, throw it away and start over."
— *Alfred Edward Perlman*

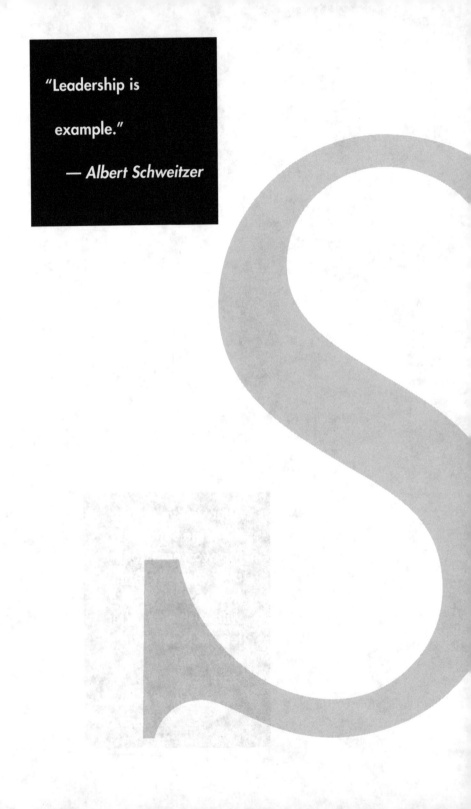

"Leadership is

example."

— *Albert Schweitzer*

"S" IS FOR STEERING TEAM

A steering team — also called a guidance team or a quality council — is the most critical component in any team-driven organization. The steering team is a group of people (not all management types!) who yearn to push power, knowledge, information, and rewards downward in the organization. They are the life force that runs interference for and empowers other teams. They act as the sun in the solar system. They give off energy to other planets (teams) so they can work and grow.

Steering team members can be elected or appointed. They can be rotated or they can be permanent. The form that the organization gives to the steering team is not as important as the fact that it is perceived by everyone in the organization as a force for positive change.

Here are some critical personality characteristics for steering team members to possess:

- A strong belief in the idea of employee involvement
- A desire for continuous learning and improvement
- A willingness to hear and search out creative ideas
- The ability to concentrate on critical issues within the organization — not trivial ones
- The ability to interact effectively with all people in the organization

Because everyone in the organization will be closely watching the steering team and looking to it for guidance, the steering team must:

- Work with employees to decide what the organization should become.

- Focus on providing quality customer service — not entirely on cutting costs and saving money or time.
- Show a definite willingness to question every existing paradigm within the organization.
- Help all employees with problem-solving skills.
- Let workers make the changes they suggest within realistic boundaries.
- Reward employees for improving the organization.
- Keep workers informed on the success or failure of quality programs within the organization and outside of the organization.
- Stay actively involved with all empowered teams. Be a coach, mentor, and facilitator and offer support for them.

The days of the "Lone Ranger Mentality" are dead. No one rides into town, fixes all the ills, and rides off into the sunset anymore. It doesn't work that way.

Effective leadership today means involving all people in the process. It means acting as a servant to bring out the best in the people around you. Sure, it's not as easy as being dictatorial, but it's what the workplace of today demands.

"If at first you don't

succeed, you're

running about

average."

— *M.H. Alderson*

"Change: the only

thing that brings

progress."

— *Charles F. Kettering*

"T" IS FOR TRANSFORMERS, TRANSMITTERS OF THE STATUS QUO, AND TREE-HUGGERS

Recently, the chief executive officer of a very successful small software company on the East Coast gathered all seventy-two of his employees together to update them on the status of the company. After awhile, he shifted his remarks to talking about the company's future.

He looked at the employees and said: "There are four kinds of people in this room. The first kind of employee will embrace the new philosophy of quality through teamwork and meet his goals. We will keep that person. The second kind of employee will embrace quality through teamwork and not meet his goals. We will keep that person too, and we will coach him or her. The third kind of employee will not embrace the quality-through-teamwork philosophy and not meet his goals. We will ask that person to leave and find another place of employment. The fourth kind of person will truly test our mettle. That individual will not embrace the quality-through-teamwork philosophy and still meet his goals. We will also ask that person to look for employment elsewhere!"

This visionary CEO felt the need to shake up his troops. He needed to let them know that although they were doing fine now, they would have to work more as a team to continue thriving. He understands that successful people often forget quickly and learn slowly.

This CEO's direct kind of leadership (with the support of the entire steering team) was designed to bring together the three key types of personalities that various participants exhibit on all teams. Let's examine these three types.

The Transformer is a person who loves change and thrives on interaction. The Transformer is very optimistic about the team's power and vision. He or she exudes optimism and feels the team can solve any problem or overcome any obstacle. Obviously, this person's energy is a real asset to the team; he or she wants to get things done. This person's weakness is a tendency to be impatient. During discussions in team meetings, the Transformer often does not think things through. This person often hurries the process too much.

The Transmitter of the status quo is a person who likes things the way they currently are. This person's motto is: "If it ain't broke, don't fix it!" The Transmitter has a steady and amiable personality and realizes that it is his or her role to steady the team and not let it do anything too rash. The Transmitter's weakness perhaps is too much complacency. He or she really doesn't care for change but can be persuaded to change.

The Tree-Hugger is someone who is totally negative toward teams. In fact, he or she may even undermine and attempt to destroy the philosophy of quality through teamwork. The Tree-Hugger is the complainer, the doomsayer — the person who drags down the entire work force. Whereas the Transformer and the Transmitter are vital players in the team's process of striking the balance and creating a win/win consensus, a Tree-Hugger has little to offer.

The CEO on the East Coast wanted to bolster and motivate his Transformers and Transmitters. He also wanted to ferret out his Tree-Huggers.

The CEO's direct approach — firing — is one possible way to deal with Tree-Huggers. Another possible solution is to help the person change his or her attitude through intensive educational effort. Sometimes enough reading, videos, or seminars can convince a Tree-Hugger to change his or her ways.

Many people advocate putting Tree-Huggers in charge of the team — giving them power and making them responsible for the success of a certain project. This is called "paradoxing the Tree-Hugger with power." Sometimes this forces the Tree-Hugger to examine the process of teamwork and totally buy into the concept of teams.

Other people recommend the "zoysia grass technique." Zoysia grass is a creeping perennial grass that takes over other types of plants (including weeds) and kills them. This technique implies that positive people will surround the Tree-Hugger on a team and bombard him or her with positive statements and support. Hopefully, this feedback will give the Tree-Hugger's self-esteem a boost, and he or she will become more of a team player.

It would, of course, be nice if all people could be molded into team players. Unfortunately, this is not the case. Getting people to change is difficult, sometimes painful, and sometimes not worth the effort.

Indeed, today's leaders must evolve their organizations by working with the people on the leading edge. Those who can catch up with the leading edge will do so. Those who cannot will probably move on.

> "The art of progress is to preserve order amid change and to preserve change amid order."
> — Alfred North Whitehead

"A gossip is one who talks to you about others; a bore is one who talks to you about himself; and a brilliant conversationalist is one who talks to you about yourself."
— Lisa Kirk

"U" IS FOR
UNDERSTANDING
THROUGH LISTENING

Listening is a valued commodity. Recent research suggests that the three most valued skills (ranked in order of importance) in the American workplace are:

1. The ability to set priorities and manage time.
2. The ability to organize and plan essential tasks.
3. The ability to listen effectively.

Likewise, listening is crucial to the success of teams. Many teams list listening constructively as one of their ground rules (see "B" for "Boundaries"). Here are some of the key characteristics of effective listeners within a team environment.

First, they practice *solid eye communication*. They make a conscious effort to maintain solid eye contact for approximately 60 percent of the time during any verbal exchange with another person. In other words, their eyes are not darting from here to there while another team member is speaking. They are not shuffling papers while another person is talking. Their eyes demonstrate that they are aware, focused, and immersed in the topic at hand. Thoreau said, "The eyes are the window to the soul." Good listeners know that and exhibit it.

Second, they practice *good body posture*. They tend to lean slightly forward as other team members present their point of view. The excellent listener encourages with his or her body posture. It has been said that Eleanor Roosevelt practiced listening to others so diligently that she would actually break into a sweat. Indeed, active listening is hard work.

75

Third, a good listener *does not interrupt* another team member. He or she waits until the speaker has finished and asks probing questions that encourage more feedback, validate the other team member, and help clarify the issue. He or she uses open-ended questions that begin with either who, what, how, when, where, or why. These are the types of questions to which another team member cannot answer "yes" or "no." The finest of all open-ended questions is simply: "What is your opinion?"

Fourth, a good listener *takes notes*. He or she has a pad and paper nearby to jot down critical phrases, words, and numbers. A good listener doesn't rely on memory to recall critical pieces of vital team data.

Listening intently doesn't necessarily mean that you agree with a fellow team member's viewpoint. Robert Frost, the great American poet, once said, "Education is the ability to listen to almost anything without losing your temper or your self-confidence." Indeed, a hallmark of superior teams is superior listening skills.

"Nobody has ever

listened themselves

out of a job."

— *Calvin Coolidge*

> "No extraordinary
>
> power should be
>
> lodged in one
>
> individual."
>
> — *Thomas Paine*

"V" IS FOR VOTING IS NOT ALLOWED

Consensus is critical for empowered teams. The "majority rules" concept has its place — but not on empowered teams; consensus must be the norm.

Critics of consensus often say, "It's too slow" or "It's not necessary." But gaining consensus among team members sends clear messages to everyone on the team. It clearly communicates these ideas:

1. No matter what your rank in the organization, we value your brain.

2. We believe that by practicing the win/win notion of consensus, we will make a better decision.

3. Decisions that are agreed upon by everyone will be more fully implemented. Indeed, people support what they create.

4. Although consensus takes more time than "top-down" decision-making, we are willing to invest that time. Yes, our organization believes that thoughtfulness (gained from consensus) is better than panic (let's shoot from the hip).

Saturn Automobiles, a phenomenal American success story, has reduced its layers of management from fifty-six to three through the efforts of empowered teams. The empowered teams make decisions by using the "70 percent comfortable" rule of consensus. This rule really implies something basic and important about the notion of seeking consensus. It implies that all team members must continue discussing the issue at hand until there is a feeling of win/win among all members of the team, much like the process a jury uses to arrive at a verdict.

79

Joseph Rypkowski of Saturn says: "All you have to do is tell somebody that once. They hear that, and they're going to hold you to it. Once you make that statement, you better be prepared to follow through because people take it very seriously."

The bottom-line lesson here is this: Take straw votes, discuss fervently, adjourn for a bit to let things incubate if you must, but get consensus. The patience exhibited by such pioneers as Saturn should serve as a true role model for us all.

"There are three sides to every

story — yours, mine, and all that

lie between."

— *Jody Kern*

"Everything we do must start out with a recognition of a balance between work and family. The only sustainable competitive advantage a company has is its employees."

— Jerre Stead
CEO of National
Cash Register

"W" IS FOR WHOLE PERSON

Truly empowered teams concern themselves with the whole individual. One large manufacturing firm in California has allowed its teams to tackle issues that affect employees outside the workplace.

Jack, the coach of one team in the facility, says: "It was truly amazing. For four-and-a-half years, my team had its ups and downs. We showed flashes of brilliance at times, and we were lackadaisical at other times. Then — whammo! Upper-level management issued a memo that encouraged our teams to address issues outside of work as well as issues inside the workplace. That memo truly turned my team on. The transformation was incredible. Our productivity as a team nearly doubled."

Jack continued with his story by saying, "When upper-level management realized that they had truly empowered us, I asked my boss why they widened our boundaries and allowed us to discuss stuff outside the four walls of work. He replied, 'We decided that our job was not to make people better employees. Our job was to make employees better people.'"

Jack summarized his story by saying: "We agreed as a team to never work more than 50 hours a week. We all have families and flex-time was already in place. We presented this concept to our steering team and they approved it. From that moment on, every team member has pulled together. We work smarter and more diligently than we ever have before. The buy-in from people has been like nothing I have ever witnessed in my seventeen years of working here!"

As the year 2000 approaches, cutting-edge organizations that want to recruit and keep good people will address the issue of balancing work and family. The best vehicle for addressing this ever-present issue is empowered teams.

"Commandment Number
One of any truly civilized
society is this: Let people
be different."
— *David Grayson*

"X" IS FOR XENOPHOBIA

Xenophobia is a fear and hatred of strangers and foreigners, or a fear and hatred of anything strange or foreign. The United States used to be considered the world's melting pot. The better and more descriptive metaphor today is this: The United States is a colorful and never-ending mosaic of diverse peoples.

Employers must view this diversity as a competitive advantage and encourage it. Hand pick teams if you must — blur the lines of bureaucracy! Ensure that teams are characterized by people with divergent points of view, different colors of skin, different ranks, and so forth.

It is through this process of cross-fertilization that individuals grow. When individuals grow, teams grow. When teams grow, organizations grow. When organizations grow, the country flourishes.

Yes, this may sound oversimplistic. But consider this: The notion of better quality through teams may be the key single ingredient that sustains many organizations into the twenty-first century.

According to Robert Solow, an M.I.T. (Massachusetts Institute of Technology) professor and 1987 Nobel Prize winner in economics, America's falling productivity is rooted in an increasingly inequitable distribution of wealth.

He states: "Although there was a substantial increase in the national income in the past 15 years, less than nothing of it went to the lowest 20 percent of families. . . . There's slower progress overall and fewer people are sharing in it."

Solow says the only way to balance the economic scales is to improve the earning power of the poor. Indeed, practice less xenophobia and improve the earning power of the less educated and less skilled people.

He believes we must elevate the average level of education and training in order to improve productivity across the United States and raise the average standard of living. We will need to do this in order to remain competitive in an increasingly competitive world.

The challenge to address the fear of anything strange or foreign lies before all of us. We must reach out and take people in.

"Change your thoughts and you change your world."

— Norman Vincent Peale

Y

"Y" IS FOR
"YES WITHIN 90 DAYS"

Success breeds success. Within ninety days of a team's inception, a team must find a success (a Yes!) and magnify it.

Even if it's a very small success, it still needs to be magnified. It's much like rolling a snowball downhill. A team's small success will help it gather momentum and solidify it as a productive working unit. This small success will serve as a catalyst for bigger and better things to come.

Donna, a team leader from Missouri, was looking diligently for a small success to give her team momentum. Her team had not been as productive as she would have liked, so she asked the head of her governmental agency if her team could provide the entertainment for the upcoming Christmas party.

After getting approval, she asked her team of six to put on a humorous skit for the party. The team members jumped at the chance! They had a good time poking fun at several fellow employees and their idiosyncrasies. They sang, gave away gag gifts, and had a great time. Donna and her team were proud of the pictures and stories that appeared in the January issue of the newsletter.

Donna said: "This skit really pulled us together. In January and February, we went on to address some challenging issues that needed taking care of. I had to travel most of the month of March, and my team made some great progress without me being there. I was truly proud of them."

It is now Christmas time again (one year later), and Donna's team is preparing the Christmas skit again. She goes on to say, "We will have fun with this skit again but, more important, my team is discussing the difficult issue of how to handle the cross-training of fellow team members."

As a successful coach of her team, Donna made something positive occur within ninety days and magnified it. As others within the organization observed the by-product of the team's labor, the team pulled together. Softly magnifying a team's accomplishments often serves as the catalyst for a team's ultimate success.

"... If one advances confidently in the direction of his dreams, and endeavors to live the life which he has imagined, he will meet with success unexpected in common hours."

— *Henry David Thoreau*

"Leadership is the capacity to

translate vision into reality."

— *Warren G. Bennis*

"Z" is for Zeal

Organizations cannot be transformed without effective leadership. The leadership within organizations needs to be extremely committed to the concept of empowered teams.

Yes, there needs to be leadership with vision; people do get excited when they can see themselves in some sort of vision. Most assuredly, leaders need to have a sense of mission. A sense of overall mission and mission statements within an organization serve as the bridge between "I wish" and "I will." Visions are worthless unless an accompanying sense of mission is attached to these future visions. Most important, a leader today needs these two items in his or her kit bag of success:

1. A passion for the team concept
2. A deep-rooted faith that the organization will change, grow, and thrive

The word *zeal* comes to mind here. Zeal is an eager and ardent interest in the pursuit of something. It means enthusiasm and passion. Yes, a team leader must be a person with a sense of passion and a deep-rooted faith in himself or herself and in others.

Successful organizations of the future will be run by high-powered leaders. The leaders of organizations that survive and thrive into the twenty-first century will be aptly described as zealous and enthusiastic coaches. These coaches will push knowledge, power, information, and rewards downward in the system. They will remove obstacles for empowered teams. They will bash barriers within organizations. They will provide equipment, training, and facilities for teams. They will not just "get the workers to do their job." They will see themselves as working for the workers — effectively serving the members of teams.

93

These leaders, or coaches, will view themselves as facilitators. The word *facilitate* emanates from the word *facile*, which means "to make easy." A coach will have a passion for serving others before he serves himself. Furthermore, a coach will also have a sense of conviction or faith. The coach believes that he or she will always be valuable and employable as a coach, servant, and facilitator.

The change of role from traditional supervisor to coach (see "A" for "Alignment") is much easier said than done. There is security in the old model of supervisor. There is ambiguity and uncertainty in the new model of coach.

Don, a plant manager in Louisiana, once said: "We continue to put supervisors in a pinched position. They get flak from upper-level management. They get flak from people they supervise. Now, we come along and tell them they are not supervisors anymore — they are coaches. Then we don't define what a coach should look like, act like, or feel like. Middle managers and supervisors need more training than anyone else in the quality movement. We cannot put them at the 'pinch point' and ask them to be coaches without supporting and training them."

These words of wisdom ring true. In order to become effective coaches, people need continual training and support. Without a doubt, a leader or coach must first begin by accepting the notions of vision and mission. However, a leader is someone who must take a leap of faith. A leader is someone who transcends the concept of coach. A leader is a person whose sparks of enthusiasm flow out of the pores of his or her skin. This leap cannot be made without a sense of passion for the organization and the people within it. This leap must also be accompanied by a ceaseless commitment to teaching and learning through empowered teams.

"The famous sixth-century B.C. Chinese philosopher Lao-Tzu described the role of the leader more than twenty-four centuries ago. "A leader is best when people barely know he exists, not so good when people obey and acclaim him, worse when they despise him... But of a good leader, who talks little, when his work is done, his aim fulfilled, they will say: We did this ourselves."

"Excellence is to do a

common thing in an

uncommon way."

— *Booker T. Washington*

A Checklist From A to Z

As you help lead your team through the points of discussion presented in this book, use this checklist to make sure you have followed through and done your job completely.

"*A*" is for Alignment. Has the organization been realigned appropriately to accommodate the new structure of our empowered teams?

"*B*" is for Boundaries. Has upper-level management clearly defined the boundaries for the empowered team(s) to operate effectively? Has each empowered team set its own set of ground rules?

"*C*" is for Creativity. Has a proper environment been created in which empowered teams can exercise their creative potential?

"*D*" is for Desired Size. Does the size of all of our teams make sense?

"*E*" is for Empowerment. Does each team feel empowered to recreate the organization and create folklore?

"*F*" is for Food and Fun. Do we ensure that our teams are experiencing the social side of teamwork — food and fun?

"*G*" is for Geese. Do we strive to have all of our teams fully function as a superior unit — such as a flock of geese would interact with one another?

"*H*" is for Humor. Are our teams infused with an ample balance of humor, laughter, and playfulness as they go about achieving their tasks?

"I" is for Impasse. Do all of our team members grasp how to get everyone past the point of impasse so the team can effectively cohere and continue working together?

"J" is for Journey. Do all team members understand the process of forming, storming, norming, performing, and disbanding?

"K" is for Keep the Focus on Results. Do all team members perceive the importance of focusing on results and not on activities through the process of RM-SMART goals?

"L" is for Levels of Communication. Do all of our team members clearly understand the four levels of communication? Do all team members understand the importance of creating a "safe" environment in which people can express themselves at the level they wish?

"M" is for Meetings. Do all team members comprehend the importance of convening focused meetings by using the SLAP concept?

"N" is for Never Backing Up. Do all team members understand the importance of never backing up, of evolving — rather than scrapping — the empowered team movement?

"O" is for Outside Observers. Do all members of the team perceive that it is okay for outside observers to observe the team and give vital feedback?

"P" is for Performance Appraisal. Do all members of the team comprehend that traditional performance appraisals do not necessarily coincide with the process of empowered teams?

"Q" is for the Quality Movement. Do all members of the empowered team understand the four components of the Quality Movement?

"R" is for Rewards. Do team members understand that changing to an empowered team movement means that the reward system within the organization may need to be reexamined?

"S" is for Steering Team. Do all team members understand the notion of the steering team and how it serves to guide and support empowered teams?

"T" is for Transformers, Transmitters of the Status Quo, and Tree-Huggers. Are all team members aware of the three distinct types of personalities that can exist on an empowered team?

"U" is for Understanding Through Listening. Are the empowered team members able to exhibit the four components of active listening?

"V" is for Voting Is Not Allowed. Do the members of the team comprehend the critical importance of reaching consensus in relation to vital team issues?

"W" is for Whole Person. Do the empowered team players realize that empowered teams within cutting-edge organizations concern themselves with the whole person — not just the person as an employee?

"X" is for Xenophobia. Do all team members grasp the notion of xenophobia and how critically important it is to allow diverse ideas to be expressed?

"Y" is for Yes Within 90 Days. Do empowered team members remember that it's critical for a team to experience at least a small success within 90 days after it forms?

"Z" is for Zeal. Do empowered team members realize the importance of a leader who coaches with enthusiasm and zeal?

AVAILABLE FROM SKILLPATH PUBLICATIONS

Self-Study Sourcebooks

Climbing the Corporate Ladder: What You Need to Know and Do to Be a Promotable Person *by Barbara Pachter and Marjorie Brody*

Coping With Supervisory Nightmares: 12 Common Nightmares of Leadership and What You Can Do About Them *by Michael and Deborah Singer Dobson*

Defeating Procrastination: 52 Fail-Safe Tips for Keeping Time on Your Side *by Marlene Caroselli, Ed.D.*

Discovering Your Purpose *by Ivy Haley*

Going for the Gold: Winning the Gold Medal for Financial Independence *by Lesley D. Bissett, CFP*

Having Something to Say When You Have to Say Something: The Art of Organizing Your Presentation *by Randy Horn*

Info-Flood: How to Swim in a Sea of Information Without Going Under *by Marlene Caroselli, Ed.D.*

The Innovative Secretary *by Marlene Caroselli, Ed.D.*

Letters & Memos: Just Like That! *by Dave Davies*

Mastering the Art of Communication: Your Keys to Developing a More Effective Personal Style *by Michelle Fairfield Poley*

Organized for Success! 95 Tips for Taking Control of Your Time, Your Space, and Your Life *by Nanci McGraw*

A Passion to Lead! How to Develop Your Natural Leadership Ability *by Michael Plumstead*

P.E.R.S.U.A.D.E.: Communication Strategies That Move People to Action *by Marlene Caroselli, Ed.D.*

Productivity Power: 250 Great Ideas for Being More Productive *by Jim Temme*

Promoting Yourself: 50 Ways to Increase Your Prestige, Power, and Paycheck *by Marlene Caroselli, Ed.D.*

Proof Positive: How to Find Errors Before They Embarrass You *by Karen L. Anderson*

Risk-Taking: 50 Ways to Turn Risks Into Rewards *by Marlene Caroselli, Ed.D. and David Harris*

Speak Up and Stand Out: How to Make Effective Presentations *by Nanci McGraw*

Stress Control: How You Can Find Relief From Life's Daily Stress *by Steve Bell*

The Technical Writer's Guide *by Robert McGraw*

Total Quality Customer Service: How to Make It Your Way of Life *by Jim Temme*

Write It Right! A Guide for Clear and Correct Writing *by Richard Andersen and Helene Hinis*

Your Total Communication Image *by Janet Signe Olson, Ph.D.*

Handbooks

The ABC's of Empowered Teams: Building Blocks for Success *by Mark Towers*

Assert Yourself! Developing Power-Packed Communication Skills to Make Your Points Clearly, Confidently, and Persuasively *by Lisa Contini*

Breaking the Ice: How to Improve Your On-the-Spot Communication Skills
by Deborah Shouse

The Care and Keeping of Customers: A Treasury of Facts, Tips, and Proven Techniques for Keeping Your Customers Coming BACK! *by Roy Lantz*

Challenging Change: Five Steps for Dealing With Change *by Holly DeForest and Mary Steinberg*

Dynamic Delegation: A Manager's Guide for Active Empowerment *by Mark Towers*

Every Woman's Guide to Career Success *by Denise M. Dudley*

Grammar? No Problem! *by Dave Davies*

Great Openings and Closings: 28 Ways to Launch and Land Your Presentations With Punch, Power, and Pizazz *by Mari Pat Varga*

Hiring and Firing: What Every Manager Needs to Know *by Marlene Caroselli, Ed.D. with Laura Wyeth, Ms.Ed.*

How to Be a More Effective Group Communicator: Finding Your Role and Boosting Your Confidence in Group Situations *by Deborah Shouse*

How to Deal With Difficult People *by Paul Friedman*

Learning to Laugh at Work: The Power of Humor in the Workplace *by Robert McGraw*

Making Your Mark: How to Develop a Personal Marketing Plan for Becoming More Visible and More Appreciated at Work *by Deborah Shouse*

Meetings That Work *by Marlene Caroselli, Ed.D.*

The Mentoring Advantage: How to Help Your Career Soar to New Heights *by Pam Grout*

Minding Your Business Manners: Etiquette Tips for Presenting Yourself Professionally in Every Business Situation *by Marjorie Brody and Barbara Pachter*

Misspeller's Guide *by Joel and Ruth Schroeder*

Motivation in the Workplace: How to Motivate Workers to Peak Performance and Productivity *by Barbara Fielder*

NameTags Plus: Games You Can Play When People Don't Know What to Say *by Deborah Shouse*

Networking: How to Creatively Tap Your People Resources *by Colleen Clarke*

New & Improved! 25 Ways to Be More Creative and More Effective *by Pam Grout*

Power Write! A Practical Guide to Words That Work *by Helene Hinis*

The Power of Positivity: Eighty ways to energize your life *by Joel and Ruth Schroeder*

Putting Anger to Work For You *by Ruth and Joel Schroeder*

Reinventing Your Self: 28 Strategies for Coping With Change *by Mark Towers*

Saying "No" to Negativity: How to Manage Negativity in Yourself, Your Boss, and Your Co-Workers *by Zoie Kaye*

The Supervisor's Guide: The Everyday Guide to Coordinating People and Tasks *by Jerry Brown and Denise Dudley, Ph.D.*

Taking Charge: A Personal Guide to Managing Projects and Priorities *by Michal E. Feder*

Treasure Hunt: 10 Stepping Stones to a New and More Confident You! *by Pam Grout*

A Winning Attitude: How to Develop Your Most Important Asset! *by Michelle Fairfield Poley*

For more information, call 1-800-873-7545.

NOTES

NOTES

NOTES

NOTES